Coffee With Ray

by

Nick Ambrosino

Also by Nick Ambrosino

Lessons With Matt

Coffee With Ray

by

Nick Ambrosino

www.nickambrosino.com

Published by Nick Ambrosino

Copyright © 2014 by Nick Ambrosino

All rights reserved

This book is licensed for your personal enjoyment only. This book may not be re-sold or given away to other people. If you would like to share this book with another person, please purchase an additional copy for each recipient. If you're reading this book and did not purchase it, or it was not purchased for your use only, then please return to amazon.com and purchase your own copy. Thank you for respecting the hard work of this author.

First Edition: 2014

Second Edition: 2015

Printed by CreateSpace

Printed in the United States of America

ISBN-13: 978-1484885451

ISBN-10: 1484885457

About the Author

A recognized music instructor, master mentor, and learning specialist, Nick Ambrosino began his career in 1986 in Bay Shore Long Island, where he taught grades K-12 music in the public school system. During that time, he began to develop his own approach to the mastery of music and learning.

He has always found teaching music simple, but facilitating an individual through the course of learning music a much more complex matter. For Nick, learning the language of music is a metaphor for learning about one's self.

"With appropriate guidance, as students learn about music they, more importantly, learn how to grow as a person. They learn how to utilize effective strategies and tools to navigate and overcome the inevitable obstacles that are on every path of study. Mastery of these strategies will ensure their success and ultimately lead to increased self-esteem and fulfillment," Nick said.

Nick is the founder and director of Music Simply Music, Long Island's leading, in-H.O.M.E. (Hands On Music Experience™) music-education program. Known for his unwavering commitment to excellence and success in his teaching, Nick continues to lead a growing team of Music Simply Music facilitators, set on providing the life-long gift of music and learning to students of all ages across Long Island.

Nick's first foray into writing occurred in 1996 when he launched Music Teacher's Insightful Practices (M-TIPS), an on-line monthly newsletter available to music teachers throughout the world. Nick's blog, which can be found at www.musicsimplymusic.com/blog, offers students and parents useful and motivational tips for attaining their musical and personal goals.

Nick Ambrosino received a Bachelor of Fine Arts in Music Education in 1985 from Long Island University, C.W. Post. He currently resides in Nesconset, New York, with his wife and three children.

Contact

Nick Ambrosino is available for speaking engagements, and educational and business consultations. He can be reached at nick@musicsimplymusic.com.

Diamond Distinctions™ and G.U.T.™ are registered trademarks of Nick Ambrosino.

Dedication

This book is dedicated to every teacher, parent, and student who has ever struggled to become, or assisted others in becoming, how they see themselves in their highest light. It is dedicated to the greatness in all of us that knows we have so much more to offer the world.

VIII

Acknowledgements

Coffee With Ray has taken a lifetime to write, well at least the lifetime of a forty-nine-year-old man! In that lifetime, many people have contributed to the inspiration and lessons; my heartfelt "Thank you" to each of you.

Thank you to Og Mandino, whom I regret never having personally met, but whom I feel I have gotten to know through his wonderfully inspirational books. It was with great hope and encouragement that I learned he did not write his first book until roughly the same age I have chosen to write mine. *The Greatest Miracle in the World* was one of the first books I read that exposed me to an entirely different way of considering my life.

Thank you to my editor, master educator, and "inspirationalist" Angela Canino. Not only have you impacted the lives of thousands of students, your love and support in this process of birthing my first book was always nurturing, fun, and inspiring. Thank you for your skill, support, trust in the process, and willingness to read and re-read and edit over and over again.

Thank you to my dear friend and confidant, Jim Conner. See what you get with persistence (yours!)? It only took ten years of diner dinners to convince me I had something worth saying. Your support, guidance, and never-failing belief in me are more than I could ever have asked for. Beyond these, however, it is your unconditional friendship, for which I am most grateful. It is something I hold of incalculable value in my life.

Thank you to every teacher with whom I have taught and who has taught me. Some have shown me what I wanted; others have shown me what I didn't want. Both were invaluable to my development as a professional educator.

Thank you to my greatest example of a true master teacher, my father. You set the stage for me when I was very young. The respect and admiration your students extended to you were the single motivating force that encouraged me to become an educator. I vividly recall walking around my junior high school feeling like the "big man on campus" because it was the same school in which you taught chorus and had a following of students who first called you "Mr. Ambrosino," then "Mr. A" and finally, with much affection, "Uncle Phil." To quote a wonderful song by Dan Fogelberg, "Your blood runs through my instrument and your song is in my soul," as it always will be. I love you.

To Angelo Truglio, you shared with me how to think differently about music education and education in general. Your concern for the person before the musician was the basis for my philosophy of teaching. I was fortunate, through your mentoring, to have been exposed to these concepts and ideas extremely early in my career, long before my cement had "hardened." For this, I am grateful.

I have a very special gratitude to anyone who has sat, shared, and debated with me through a porch, arbor, or cappuccino session. Thank you for allowing me the chance to flesh out my ideas and explore them with you. Your willingness to listen and challenge me was paramount in assisting in the clarification of which concepts worked and which needed further exploration.

Thank you to all my students. While you may not have known it at the time, our lessons were my laboratory and each of you *my* teacher! Just as you were learning, so was I. I was learning what worked for you and what didn't. I was learning what worked for *me* and what didn't! We were both students and we were both teachers.

Thank you to my wonderful family. To my three children, the language of the written word simply does not have the symbols to express how I feel about you. To simply tell you I am proud is a gross understatement. You have challenged me, frustrated me, and encouraged me but, most of all, through everything, as has your mother, you have loved me. No words can express how I feel, but the look and tears of pride in my eyes always will. I love you.

And finally, to my wife, Diane, you have always been the gentleness to my serious nature, the compassion to my stubbornness. You provide me with balance and joy and continue to model the one concept I am still learning, the ability to simply relax. Thank you for putting up with my "wars of words" and my unforgiving nature to communicate exactly and properly. I fully understand how difficult this can be for everyone in my life; it's just that you have chosen to live with me through it! I adore you.

Chapter 1

What a day—eleven students and no break. I had two students who practiced and, for the rest, I was a "musical babysitter." Is this what eighteen years of musical experiences, including fourteen years of private lessons, a degree in music education, and countless performances in almost every genre of music have turned into?

These are days when I wish I just made pizza. You make a pizza, someone buys the pizza, and someone eats the pizza. It's simple. No one cares if the person buying the pizza practiced eating pizza that week. The person buying didn't have to be motivated to become a better pizza buyer and eater during the week. The buyer didn't need to have his self-esteem stroked and coddled in order to feel like eating pizza. The buyer didn't need to have someone remind him on a daily basis to make sure he practiced the pizza consumption game! Pizza is simple. Teaching is not.

Sometimes teaching simply sucks. I can't imagine that the pizza maker gets frustrated with himself for messing up a pizza. I can't imagine that he stands

NOTES:

in front of his pizza-making station and wonders how on earth he's going to turn this lump of dough, pile of mozzarella, and bowl of tomato sauce into a pizza. But that's what I have to do.

There are days I arrive at my lessons to a ball of dough that not only isn't yet in pizza form but, in some ways, actually resists becoming a pizza. I've had it with this job. Why couldn't I have chosen a different career? Maybe one in which I really didn't care about what I did, a job where I could make enough money to pay my bills, save some cash, and then have other interests? At least then, I could go home and just leave it "at the office."

But no, I chose to do what I loved; I chose to share music, my music, their music, the music of the world, with others. I chose it with little regard for the money it would or wouldn't make me. I chose it because people told me, "If you can make a career out of what you love, you'll never work a day in your life." What a load of crap! If you make a career out of what you love, you'll start to hate what you once loved.

I don't make music much anymore. When I get home from teaching, the last thing I want to do is hear more music. I used to listen to every style of music you could imagine. My music collection has Aerosmith, AC/DC, Amos Lee, Anita Baker, Babyface, Bach, Bill Evans, Bob Marley, Bobby McFerrin, Brahms, Chick Corea, Chet Baker, Chopin, The Doobie Brothers, Ella Fitzgerald, Antonio Carlos Jobin, Carlos Santana, The Meters,

NICK AMBROSINO

Mozart, Paul Simon, The Rolling Stones, Weather Report, and Yo-Yo Ma. And the list could go on! My music collection has over 10,000 different songs from every style and artist you could imagine.

I just don't want to hear more music after hearing music all day. It's like a baker going home and someone serving him donuts and cake! I once read that Debussy said music was made up of both sound and silence and most composers do not know how to use the latter of those two. Well, I guess life is the same way. I have so much "sound" in my day that, at the end of it, I'm only interested in hearing silence. Actually, the only time I go to my instrument to actually play it, is when the day is absolutely *horrible*. When the day is that *bad* I either play loudly to vent my frustration (which is not really making beautiful music, most teachers would call it "banging"), or I play beautifully to remember what music, real music, is supposed to sound like. Most of the time, I just play loudly.

Most of my forty-five students are school-aged kids, so my work hours begin when they come home from school. I teach five days a week, from around three to nine, depending on the day, which means that, for the most part, I eat just before I go to sleep, at the unhealthiest time to fuel my body. It's another reason I hate what I do. If tomorrow is going to be another today, cash me out now. Let me off the boat. I don't want another fifty years of this!

NOTES:

NOTES:

COFFEE WITH RAY

At about midnight, after watching a couple of episodes of Seinfeld, I fall asleep on the couch.

Chapter 2

NOTES:

I was awakened around 6:30 AM by my neighbor's barking dog. Actually, it was 6:12 when the barking had started, and I opened my eyes to look at the alarm. Inconsiderate SOB! She didn't take the dog in until 6:35 and by then the barking had me fully awake, fully frustrated, and I hadn't even started teaching!

Since it was the middle of January and it was snowing, I couldn't go out for a ride on my bike so, instead, I simply made my morning cappuccino and checked in with the local television station. There was going to be more snow with the temperature rising just enough, by midday, to change the precipitation to rain, enough to make it gray, wet, and ugly. After the news started repeating itself, I turned the TV off and read more of my Nelson DeMille novel. I must have been tired, because I fell asleep on the couch, still in my pajamas, for about an hour.

Before showering, I exercised to burn off last night's crappy dinner. I put my bike on an indoor trainer and rode for forty-five minutes while listening to some random mix on my iPod. It's weird trying to get a good workout while riding to the second movement of Beethoven's Pathétique Sonata. But my iPod was connected to the stereo receiver, so I just let it go.

Today, because I had some adults who were retired and could take lessons before the school-aged kids got home, my teaching day started around 1:30. I don't know if I would like my career choice any better if I could only teach retired adults, but I certainly wouldn't mind getting home at five, instead of the usual nine o'clock. The bad part about starting at 1:30 was that it was just a prelude to my normal day. Instead of starting two hours earlier and *ending* two hours earlier, I simply started two hours earlier and worked longer. Today it was eleven lessons in a row. I justified it by telling myself I was making more money.

I left for my lessons a little bit earlier than usual, expecting some bad driving conditions; my expectation was accurate. What was normally a ten-minute drive to my first lesson took closer to twenty-five minutes. It was going to be a long day.

My first two lessons were easy, both adults, both okay with the fact that they "didn't have time to practice" and both completely satisfied that we would practice together. When I arrived at my 3:30 lesson, I found the driveway empty, which was odd since this client had four cars and two were always parked in the driveway.

NICK AMBROSINO

I knocked on the door and rang the bell, but it appeared that no one was home. I waited my standard fifteen minutes, tried the doorbell again, and still no one answered. I left a friendly note on the back of a business card that said, "Hope all is okay. We had a 3:30 lesson today," dated it, to prove that I had been there, and left, annoyed.

This wasn't the first time this client no-showed me. To make matters worse, it was a double lesson. Now I had an hour to kill. It's a good thing I've been doing this long enough to always keep some reading material in my car.

Usually, I would just find a parking lot and read, but the weather was getting more brutal. The temperature had, in fact, warmed to that magical thirty-four degrees; not warm enough to just be raining and not cold enough to just be snowing, just ugly enough to be snaining. (It was my word for the combination of snow and rain the clouds were dumping on us. "Rowing" was already taken.)

I was chilled to the bone and, with the price of gas close to $4.00 a gallon, I didn't feel like wasting it by keeping my car heated and running for an hour. I needed to find a place I could get a decent cup of coffee that had an area to sit and read.

The strange thing was that with 20,000 Starbuck's worldwide, there wasn't one in the area I was in. Maybe I should call Starbuck's headquarters to let them know they missed a corner of the country!

NOTES:

COFFEE WITH RAY

I typed "coffee" in my GPS, which yielded several places that sold coffee beans and machines, but didn't brew coffee. Hmmm, how about "café?" Yep, that worked. There was one within five miles of my location. "Jo's Café." Good thing for GPS search functions, because I never would've come through this part of the town. Jo's Café was hidden behind a small three-store shopping area and short of being a local, Jo's was not a place you would find by just driving by. Yet, the locals must've known something because, much to my dismay, Jo's parking lot was packed at 4:00 PM on a Thursday afternoon. As I peered through the three walls of six-foot-high windows that wrapped around Jo's, I could see that the parking lot population was not an accurate representation of the customer population. There were far more people inside than there were cars outside. The place was buzzing.

Jo's was clean and well lit—a comfortable escape from the mess outside. There was a nautical theme throughout. The large bookshelf to my left looked like it was well stocked with donated books. Directly in front of me, behind the counter, and above the coffee machines was an "X" created by two crossing oars. A white circular life preserver hung where the oars crossed.

I was looking forward to sitting down and reading a book, but none of the tables were empty. There was a couple that appeared to be having a little romantic rendezvous near the window, while students, scattered throughout the various couches and tables, studied, some in groups, others alone. A table for four was occupied by a single older man typing on a computer, inconsiderate SOB, taking up all that space when there were other people who wanted to sit.

After ordering a double espresso, I turned from the line and scanned the place one more time to see if anyone had left, with no luck. I looked at the single man sitting at the quad and shook my head in disdain. As I walked to the exit, he said, without looking up, "You can sit here if you'd like."

"Excuse me?"

"You can sit in one of the chairs at this table. It's meant for four, but it was the only one available next to an outlet when I arrived."

"No, that's okay," I replied, a bit embarrassed by my initial cynical thoughts about this guy.

"Suit yourself, whatever you want," he responded.

I took one more step to the door and was quickly reminded of how crappy and cold it was going to be in my car. I turned, swallowed my pride a bit (although I didn't quite know why I felt embarrassed, I hadn't said anything rude, I had just thought it), and said, "Well, okay, if it's not an imposition, I'll take you up on your offer."

"Suit yourself, whatever you want," he said, again without looking up.

With a forced exhale, I plopped down on the chair opposite him. My back was to the door, not a position I preferred. I like to see the people who entered a store. I guess it was the ten years of martial arts that made me hyper sensitive to my surroundings and trained me to never place myself in a compromising position. Or maybe I was just neurotic. The spot on the table I would have preferred was the one this guy was in, back to the wall able to scope out the entire café at all times. My friends knew of my neurosis and always waited for me to sit first when we went out to eat. I greatly appreciated that.

As I wasn't able to monitor the flow of traffic in and out of the café, I was stuck facing him. He was typing away on an HP laptop computer plugged into the wall. Either he had a crappy battery or he had been, or was going to be there for a while. Either way, I only had to be here for the next forty-five or so minutes, as my next lesson was at 5:15.

"Tough day?" he asked as I was taking a sip of my coffee. I looked up, his blue eyes and slight smile combined to suggest a feeling of calm confidence.

I took a sip of my coffee and burned my tongue. Damn it!

"Ow! Yeah, and it just got worse!"

"Not to your liking?" he said.

"It's too hot," I replied.

"Yyyep, they tend to keep the water five degrees too hot," he responded.

NICK AMBROSINO

NOTES:

I'm a bit of an espresso snob. I have a fine Italian espresso machine at home, and I have my beans sent to me on the day they're roasted. I grind them as I need them. Beans have to be freshly ground to insure the best crema and, if the temperature of the water is too high (it should be around 205 degrees Fahrenheit), the espresso will taste burnt. It wasn't the worst I've tasted, but it certainly wasn't the best—a bit bitter, probably a northern style Italian blend.

"Oh, you like espresso, too."

"Yep," he replied again.

He was probably around sixty-five or so years old, but it wasn't the lines on his face that gave it away, it was his hands. The skin on his face looked more youthful, but hands never lie.

Being a pianist, I notice hands. As he reached for his coffee, I noticed his. They appeared to be weathered but not abused. His nails were neatly trimmed and there was a thin gold wedding ring on the pinkie of his left hand. He took a big gulp of his coffee. It must have been there for a while because he drank it without regard to its temperature.

He was wearing a dark flat cap and a light blue striped shirt. Both appeared well weathered, like a child's blanket. The collared shirt was faded and worn, but still in good shape, probably from LL Bean.

"This place is busy," I offered in small talk.

COFFEE WITH RAY

"It's not always like this, earlier in the day it's quieter, less people. The kids are in school," he replied.

"The coffee's not cheap either," I added, more small talk. "$3.50 for a double shot of espresso."

"Yep, it's $3.50 whether you like the price or not. And if you don't like the price it just makes the coffee taste bitter," he answered back.

Great, he was a damn philosopher, just what I needed on an already crappy day. I must have glared at him a bit, because he looked up with a slight nod and returned to his computer.

I took out my book, more to disconnect from this conversation than to read. With just forty minutes remaining, I figured I would be able to ignore him for the remainder of my time.

I was trying to finish all of the Nelson DeMille "John Corey" novels by the end of the year. I was on the second in the series, with three more to go. The problem was that I could never read one book at a time. I was usually reading something fictional (the DeMille novel), something biographical (Lincoln), something that stretched my comfort zone (presently that was Nassim Nicholas Taleb's *The Black Swan*—read-a-page-put-it-down-and-digest type of book) and something related to investing, usually a digitally downloaded magazine.

That's why I loved my digital reader. I didn't have to carry around four or five different books. I could carry my entire library and read whatever I was in the mood for at the time.

As I clicked to my latest bookmark, his typing and clicking distracted me. The steady rhythm punctuated by the syncopated clicks of his mouse was interspersed with the voices of people placing their orders at the counter. I guess it's the curse or blessing, depending on how you view it, of the musician. I hear sounds as they relate to other sounds in the environment. I got the idea when I saw a movie about the Bach prodigy, Glenn Gould, called *Thirty-Two Short Films about Glenn Gould*.

Glenn Gould goes into a diner, sits down, and creates a beat on his hand that ties together all the different "melodic motifs" he was hearing—the roughness of the truck driver relating a story to his friends, the clanking of pots and pans from the kitchen, the voice of the waitress, the tinkling of silverware.

I thought it was a neat way of calming my impatience by giving me something to do in undesirable situations.

My tablemate's typing was the prominent motif in my spontaneous fugue. When I looked at him, he gently smiled and nodded his approval at whatever was on the computer screen in front of him. He leaned back in his chair and clasped his hands behind his head.

I busied myself in my book and reached for my espresso without looking up.

NOTES:

COFFEE WITH RAY

After a while, I looked at my watch and realized I only had ten minutes to get to my lesson. I quickly finished the last sip of my now cold espresso, shut the cover on my e-reader, buttoned up my coat, and got up to leave.

As I walked away from the table, I shot out a quick "Goodbye," not to anyone in particular, but I guess to the man I had been sitting with. When I got to the door, I thought I heard him say, "See you soon."

I pulled my wool hat over my ears and trekked through the snain to my car. The door opened with a creak (the last time I tested it against a piano, it was an F sharp—another curse of being a musician). I ducked my head, and I slid into the leather seat. I started the car and waited a minute for the engine to warm. As I put it into reverse, my tablemate gave a brief wave.

While I sat at the light outside of Jo's, my phone rang. It was my brother from California. "Hey, bro," I answered.

"What's going on?" he replied.

"Nothing, same old, same old. How 'bout you? How's work?" I inquired.

He had recently changed jobs and was navigating the culture and politics of a new company. I knew he was stressed out and he knew my question was alluding to this.

"It is what it is," he sighed.

NICK AMBROSINO

As I was on the other side of the country, I felt badly that I couldn't provide him with more support like a drink, a bitching session, a game of golf, or whatever. "Hey, man, can I get back to you tonight or tomorrow? I'm just on my way to a lesson. Everything okay?"

"Like I said, 'It is what it is,'" he repeated.

That didn't sound good to me, but I had to teach, so I dismissed it and pretended he was okay. "All right, I'll call you later tonight or tomorrow. Take care. Love ya."

"Right back at ya," he replied and then hung up.

The rest of the day was more of the same—students who hadn't practiced, students whose housekeepers hid their music books, students who forgot everything from last week, forcing me to go back and review what I had taught them last week and the week before.

I got home around 9:30 and repeated my private music teacher's eating routine—I had two slices of pizza and a Diet Coke.

And if you don't like the price, it just makes the coffee taste bitter. Excuse me? As I drifted off to sleep on my couch, the café philosopher's words shot through my head. *And if you don't like the price, it just makes the coffee taste bitter.* Why were his words repeating themselves in my head? I woke up from my nap around 11:00 PM and transferred myself to my bed.

NOTES:

Chapter 3

I awoke on Friday at 7:30. I followed my routine of a morning cappuccino, a ride to nowhere on my stationary bike, and a shower. It was about 10:30 when I completed the morning grind, calculating the time in California to be 7:30. My brother was at work, so I called, and we caught up.

As I suspected, life was stressful, but all he really shared was, "It is what it is," one of his favorite sayings when there wasn't anything new to report, and when he just had to accept the way things were.

The rest of the day was a typical teaching day with students who hadn't practiced, parents who had forgotten about our regular every-single-Friday-for-the-past-six-months lesson time, traffic because of a local bridge closing; and S.S.D.D. (Same Stuff Different Day) as a shirt I had once seen stated. There was nothing new except for that damn phrase that kept running through my mind: *And if you don't like the price, it just makes the coffee taste bitter.*

NOTES:

COFFEE WITH RAY

The end of every Friday never comes soon enough. I always feel relieved when I arrive home at 7:30 and pour myself a cocktail. This week was only different because 7:30 was actually 8:15 due to the traffic. But, I had made it to the end of another week.

I was looking forward to the weekend because, on Saturday, I would perform at a local venue with my band, *and* because I didn't have to teach again until Monday. I enjoy the stage work because it allows me to cut loose from the more conservative image I portray when I'm teaching. The simple fact is, however, that performance work is too sporadic to earn a consistent and predictable living off the proceeds. It's a supplement to my teaching income, not a substitute.

The rest of the weekend was a blur and Monday arrived way too soon.

Chapter 4

NOTES:

Monday morning was a bit different this week, as I was attending a seminar on the Alexander method at a local piano teacher's house. The Alexander method is a method of body relaxation used by many musicians and actors to assist them in utilizing their energy in the most economical fashion. I was interested in how it could affect both my students' as well as my own playing.

The seminar was being given in a rather affluent section of the county and the host's home reflected this. Interestingly enough, I realized that it wasn't too far from Jo's Café.

The host had two Steinway concert grand pianos in her immaculate studio, which overlooked the bay. What incredible instruments and what a view!

I was one of about fifty other teachers attending, one of seven men, and certainly the youngest person in the room, by about twenty years. This should be interesting ….

The seminar was going along fine until I posed a question to the presenter who had said that for a student to be successful at the piano, they *must* have an adjustable bench.

"What if a student doesn't have an adjustable bench?" I asked.

I was sitting in the back of the room and instantly had forty plus pairs of eyes turn around and look at me with surprise. I smiled uncomfortably and was abruptly told by the presenter, "The student should not be taking piano lessons."

WHAT? If that was the case, then I shouldn't be here, as either a professional pianist or a teacher, and neither should ANY of my students because neither I nor any of my students have ever owned an adjustable bench! In the rare case I needed to adjust the height of a student's piano bench, I would just have him sit on books. The simple fact that a student wanted to play the piano was more important to me than the exact height of the piano bench. Those types of technical specifics weren't as important to me until later in a student's education.

But I said nothing, because I could see that the other participants were appalled by my question, as they nodded in agreement with the presenter.

Luckily for me, the first break was only fifteen minutes away, and I used it to quietly exit the home and the seminar.

It was about 10:30, and I had several hours to kill before my first lesson. Since my day didn't start far from where the seminar was given, I decided not to drive the forty minutes back to my home.

NICK AMBROSINO

According to my GPS I wasn't too far from Jo's, about five miles so, with my trusty e-reader in hand, I made my way. This time it was considerably less populated than on Thursday. I parked in the first spot to the right of the front door.

Upon entering, I took off my coat, hung it over my arm, and made my way to the counter to order a regular coffee. After forking over my $2.85 (which I had decided was a wonderful price for such a fine cup of Joe) I turned to look for the table that had the milk, sugar, and stirrers. As I did so, I heard someone call my name, "Hi, Matt."

I looked in front of me and there he was, the same man I had shared a table with or, more accurately, who had shared his table with me on Thursday, though I didn't recall ever sharing names.

"Oh, hi. How do you know my name?" I asked, intrigued.

He pointed to below my left shoulder, where the nametag from the seminar still read, "Hello, My Name is Matt." I took it off, feeling slightly foolish.

He extended his hand and said, "I guess it's only fair, my name is Ray."

I awkwardly extended my arm from under my coat and said, "Hello, Ray."

"No espresso today?" he asked with a smile.

"No, I really wasn't too fond of it last week. Today I'm drinking regular coffee."

NOTES:

COFFEE WITH RAY

"I understand. The espresso is brewed too hot," he reiterated from Thursday. "All coffee is best brewed just shy of boiling."

"I agree. It's nice to meet someone who appreciates the finer points of good coffee," I shared.

Upon looking at him closer, I realized that my initial impression was probably wrong. He appeared to be older than the sixty-five years I had originally estimated. He looked closer to his mid to late seventies, but with the spark in his eye of an enthusiastic twenty-five-year-old.

"I've got my table over there, if you'd like to join me," he commented as he pointed to the table in the corner, the same quad he had sat at the week prior. This time, however, he had set up his chair so that his back was to the café, leaving two of the open chairs looking out at the cafe for me. I accepted his invitation, but wondered if it was just a coincidence or if somehow he knew of my neurosis. I scooted in behind the aged wooden table, placed my coat on the inside chair, and pulled the outside chair so it was on a forty-five degree angle to the wall, allowing me to cross my right leg over my left. I took a sip of my $2.85 coffee.

"How's your coffee?" he asked.

"The best $2.85 I've spent today," I replied sarcastically.

He chuckled and raised his eyebrows. "How many other '$2.85s' have you spent today?" he poked.

NICK AMBROSINO

"Well ... about twenty-two of them."

"You've already had twenty-two cups of coffee and it's only 11:00 AM?" he asked, surprised.

"No. I just came from a seminar that cost me fifty dollars, which was a complete waste of my time. That's about twenty-two cups of coffee. I was so annoyed and frustrated, that I cut out early."

"Actually, it's somewhere between seventeen and eighteen cups," he stated matter-of-factly, as he continued to work on his computer.

"I see you teach piano lessons, is that what your seminar was about?" he inquired.

Now how could he know that? I wasn't wearing one of those cheap-looking piano ties, and I wasn't carrying a brief case that had a piano on it.

"How can you 'see' that?" I asked, again intrigued.

"Your car has a magnet on the side that says 'Piano Lessons In Your Home.' I noticed it when you drove away last week."

That's twice his simple skills of observation made me feel foolish for imparting him with superhuman powers.

"Yes, I do."

"Nice sign. I've always wanted to take lessons, but when I was younger my parents couldn't afford them."

NOTES:

COFFEE WITH RAY

Even though I had a waiting list of students, I was always trying to build my business. I said, "It's never too late to learn. I have several adult students."

He just smiled and nodded, "Maybe someday."

Ray was eating a scone; it looked like blueberry. A large coffee sat alongside his computer.

"I hope I'm not imposing upon your time," I queried.

"Not at all, I'm always on the computer. It's good to take a break and speak with someone," he said as he wrung his hands together.

There was something sad in the way he said that, something lonely, but maybe I was just projecting my own feelings upon him. Yet, it felt like there was definitely something more behind his words.

"Do you come here often?" I asked.

"Are you next going to ask me what my sign is?" he replied with a laugh and a pause. "Yes, most days. How long have you taught piano?" he asked, shifting the focus back to me.

"Seven looong years," I replied.

"Oh, you don't enjoy it?" he asked.

Suddenly, I realized the bind my flippant remark had caused me. On one hand, I had suggested he take piano lessons with me and then on the other, I didn't seem too enthusiastic about teaching. I backpedaled a bit. "Well, I sort of exaggerated. All the years haven't been long."

"I have to imagine you must have a lot of patience if you've done that for seven years," he offered as a way of saving face for me.

"I guess so," I responded, embarrassed. "Sometimes it's fun and sometimes it's not."

"Sounds like life to me. Sometimes you're the bird and sometimes you're the statue," he smiled as he said this.

"Yes, I suppose. Most of the time, though, I feel like the statue!"

He reached into his pocket and took out a small three-by-four-inch notebook and jotted something down with a wooden fountain pen he had in his left breast pocket.

"Cute notebook," I said, hoping he would offer what it was he was writing.

"Yes, it's the new rage. It's an iPad. I always carry my iPad with me wherever I go, 'cept mine stands for 'Idea Pad.' I never know when something is going to ring for me. I used to scramble for a napkin or piece of scrap paper, but that got messy and unorganized. Now I just carry my iPad with me."

Well, now I knew what the pad was for, but not what had "rung" for him.

COFFEE WITH RAY

"That's interesting," I responded, absentmindedly. I wondered if I should ask what had rung for him? Why not?

"What rang for you?" I asked, timidly.

"Oh, just that when I said to you, 'Sometimes you're the bird and sometimes you're the statue,' I realized that statues can't move out of the way of the bird, but people can," he replied.

"I never thought of it that way," I said.

"People don't have to accept what life gives them. They can choose the life they want. But most people just stand there and let the bird drop its droppings on them. They're the victims, and I understand why."

"Why would someone allow a bird to crap on them?" I asked, confused.

"Because it's a lot easier to be a victim and complain, than it is to take control of your life and change it into what you actually want," he said passionately.

"Hmm, I never really considered that." I wondered if I was the victim he described.

"It takes a lot of effort and commitment to change your life. Most people don't have the where-with-all to do it on their own and don't know how to set up a network or support system to assist them in getting to their goals. They just complain to the same friends who complain back to them."

NICK AMBROSINO

"How do you set up a support system?" I asked.

"You find someone who has what you want and then you ask them to show you how they got it. You then simply emulate, to the best of your ability and with respect to your own path, their way of thinking, and actions. No use reinventing the wheel," he declared.

I pondered his statement. He certainly had a clarity and a calmness that was enticing, and I have to admit that my "mental fish tank" was a bit cloudy these days. I was enjoying his insights and, while it was still too early to decide, I thought I liked him as well.

"Do you have more of these 'rocking chair' insights?" I asked.

"Well, if you're insinuating that I'm old …."

"No, no. I just mean that they seem so obvious I just wonder why I never thought of them. That's all," I defended.

"You never thought of them, because you're probably not really paying attention," he chided.

"What do you mean I'm not paying attention? Of course I pay attention," I defended again.

"How many times have you been to Jo's?" he asked.

"This is my second time," I replied.

NOTES:

COFFEE WITH RAY

"Have you noticed the eight-foot-long canoe hanging from the ceiling?" he asked.

I was embarrassed to admit I hadn't.

"Can we meet again?" I asked, humbled. "Will you be here tomorrow?"

"No, I won't be here tomorrow," he said.

I felt disappointed. He must have seen the look on my face.

"I won't be here tomorrow, but if you'd like, you can come by my home at ten o'clock on Wednesday. I don't live too far from Jo's, and I make a better cup of coffee," he offered.

I thought for a moment and then replied, "Okay, what's your address?"

"I can give you directions from Jo's, if you'd like," he said.

"That's okay, you can just give me the address, and I'll plug it into my GPS."

"3 Renaissance Lane. It's in Sayville."

"3 Re-nais-sance Lane, Say-ville," I replied as I typed it into my cell phone. "Do you also want to exchange numbers in case anything changes?" I asked.

"That would be fine," he replied.

I put his number in my phone and he wrote mine down on his "iPad."

NICK AMBROSINO

"See you Wednesday at 10:00 AM," I reiterated, a habit from insuring that my clients knew when I had scheduled their next lesson.

"Enjoy your day," Ray said as I left Jo's.

NOTES:

Chapter 5

I spent the next two days questioning my decision to meet Ray at his home. My mind was plagued with doubts and questions. Who was he? Why was I so easily impressed? What if he was on America's Most Wanted list? Why would I ask to meet again? I knew nothing about him, except that he appeared to know about the proper temperature for coffee brewing.

My mind was so distracted with these thoughts on Monday, that on Tuesday I decided to call him to cancel our Wednesday appointment. I dialed his number early Tuesday morning, and it just rang, no answer, no voice mail.

Later in the day, I tried twice more, once in between lessons and another on my way home, but I was disconnected on both occasions. Crappy cell phone service! By the time I had remembered to call from my home, it was too late.

Wednesday morning came and, as soon as I got up, I contemplated cancelling but thought that would

NOTES:

be rude with such short notice. Damn it, sometimes I wish I could just act irresponsibly.

Ray's house was about forty minutes east of mine and only ten minutes east of Jo's. Most of the travel to his house was semi-highway roads: speed limits of fifty-five but with lights. Once I turned off County Road 107, I entered a more residential area.

The drive through his neighborhood showed that everyone on the block appeared to take pride in their homes; they were well kempt and nicely landscaped. A light frosting of snow covered each lawn, but none was on the street, just the way I liked it. It made for a pretty winter picture where you saw the beauty but didn't feel the cold.

I arrived at Ray's house at precisely 10:00 AM. I'm a bit neurotic when it comes to time, as my business has been built upon respect for people's time. I hear countless stories about teachers showing up thirty minutes late without so much as a phone call or a reason. I've even heard stories about teachers not showing up at all. I never counted myself among the ranks of these so-called "teachers." A true teacher was a professional and acted accordingly. Sometimes I thought that all it took to be successful was to simply show up as scheduled!

With yellow siding, white trim, and smoke streaming from the chimney, Ray's house had a welcoming feel to it. It looked like a Victorian wanna-be—perhaps a house that was once smaller and was converted. I believe I had read somewhere that this neighborhood used to be a summer escape for many of the people from the metropolitan area about seventy miles west. Back in the 1940s, it contained bungalows that didn't have heat because they were only used in the summer and then boarded up for the winter.

I didn't pull into Ray's driveway, making the assumption that his car was parked in the garage, and I didn't want to get in his way should he need to pull out. I pulled next to the curb, in front of his house, another habit I had from servicing my clients in their homes.

I walked up the asphalt driveway, wet but without a layer of snow, and turned left onto the brick walkway to his front door. A dried wreath from Christmas still remained on the door. It looked like it had seen better days. I rang the bell and heard a dog charge the door, barking to alert the residents. Through the glass on the sides of the entry, I could see what appeared to be a mixed-breed animal weighing more than fifty pounds.

Before he opened the door, I heard Ray command the dog to "back up and leave it" to which the dog stopped barking and sat. Ray rewarded the dog with a pat on its head and opened the door. "Good morning, Matt," he offered.

Ray was in exercise clothes: blue sweat pants, gray hooded sweatshirt, and running shoes. The only thing that did not fit the outfit was a pink ribbon affixed to the upper left side of his sweatshirt.

COFFEE WITH RAY

"You're timing is perfect, I just got back from a 5K run."

I tentatively stepped inside and wiped my wet sneakers on the entrance mat. The dog hadn't moved from its spot but was extending his snout to catch my scent. He looked friendly; he was barely able to keep his butt down from the wagging of his tail.

"Are you afraid of dogs?" Ray asked.

"No. I'm definitely a dog person."

"This is Elvis," Ray said, introducing the dog. Elvis appeared to take this as a sign that it was okay to release from his seated position and approach me. I stood tall as he sniffed me excitedly and, once he had calmed down, I squatted to his level, at which I got a face full of dog tongue.

Elvis' welcoming manner relaxed me, and I began to feel more comfortable being at Ray's house, figuring that a nice friendly dog equaled a nice friendly owner.

"Looks like he likes you. That's a good sign. Dogs and children always know who to trust because they trust their own feelings," Ray stated.

"He's great!" I exclaimed, knowing immediately that Elvis and I would be friends. "Did you name him after the singer?" the musician in me inquired.

"Yes, but not the one I believe you're referring to," Ray replied. "He's not named after Elvis Aaron

Presley. He's named after Elvis Costello. I've always found his music and lyrics inspiring."

"What kind of dog is he?" I asked.

"He's a rescue dog from the shelter. We think he's part boxer and part Rhodesian Ridgeback," Ray answered. "I've always felt that when you put your heart out to one of the shelter dogs, they can sense that they're loved and reward their owner that much more. Certainly has been that way with Elvis. We've been together for eleven years."

"That's a long time," I responded.

"Yes, yes it is," Ray said, as he put his left hand into his right and looked off into the distance.

"Would you like a cup of coffee, Matt?"

"That would be great. Thanks."

He escorted me to a simple kitchen. A vacuum coffee pot sat waiting for water.

"Have a seat," Ray instructed.

I pulled out one of the stools that surrounded the island in the middle of the kitchen. There were already two mismatched cups from different states on the counter. One was from Paradise, Utah, and the other from Houston, Texas. Beneath the cups were mismatched saucers. I guess Ray must have guessed I would've responded "Yes" to the coffee offer, but he didn't have to be too observant to have guessed my response.

COFFEE WITH RAY

Ray freshly ground the beans and put them in the top half of the vacuum pot. A vacuum pot looks like an hourglass; it works on the expansion and contraction of gas (water vapor.) The bottom half is filled with water and heated. The water vapor travels up a tube that connects the two halves through a filter. It then exits the tube in the top half. Once the heat is removed a vacuum is created in the lower pot, which pulls the water from the top half down through the grinds and back into the bottom half. It is probably one of the purest and best-tasting cups of coffee I've ever had. It's a very sophisticated-looking way of making coffee.

"Wow, a vacuum pot. The last time I saw one of those was in a fine restaurant while I was on vacation in Miami," I stated.

"Yep. I figured you would appreciate it. To me, the best coffee is either brewed in a vacuum pot, a French press, or a Chemex pot," Ray added.

I knew all three of his references and felt well-educated and comfortable being in like-minded company.

As I sat watching him pour my coffee, I noticed he moved slowly. Not slowly in the sense of his age, but slowly in a methodical, almost planned motion. It seemed that each of his movements was pre-orchestrated. Almost like attending a Japanese Tea Ceremony.

Elvis had taken a seat by my right foot. Ray looked down and said, "Looks like you made a friend." I reached down and gave Elvis a good scratch on his head, after which he looked up and licked my hand.

Ray casually asked what appeared to be a simple question. Little was I to realize the weight of such a short query. "What do you want?"

"What?" I replied.

"What do you want?" he repeated.

"I just take cream, thank you."

"Nooo. What do you want?"

"Okay, if you don't have cream, I'll just take milk, thanks."

"Please answer my question. What do *you* want? Not 'What do you want in your coffee?'"

"What do *I* want?"

"Is there an echo in here or are you having a hard time hearing me? You're a music teacher; you're supposed to have good listening skills. I'm the older of the two of us. If anyone should have a hearing problem, it should be me."

"What do *I* want?"

"There you go again!" he said.

"I wasn't speaking to *you*, I was just saying the question out loud to myself," I snapped back.

I never really considered what I wanted. I just sort of taught. Well, I didn't just "sort of teach" I was good at it, but I wasn't having fun or feeling like I

COFFEE WITH RAY

made a difference. I just felt like any other piano teacher. I had become a parody of myself. "One and two and three and four." I actually started hearing myself say that in a lesson!

While Ray was criticizing my understanding of the English language, he had placed a small pitcher of cream on the counter. I poured some into my coffee. Actually, I poured too much, and it flowed over the edge onto the saucer and countertop. I reached for a napkin, wiped the countertop, and then placed another napkin between the cup and the saucer.

As I took a sip, I reflected on his question. I don't know if what came out of my mouth was the result of an immediate caffeine kick or if it was the unlocking of a hidden room in my personal vault but, whatever caused it, it was unexpected and alarming.

"What I want is to know that I'm having a *lifelong* impact on the people I'm teaching, and I want to feel successful while I do it. I want to have fun doing it! But I don't just want to make them better piano players; I want to assist them in being better people, people with the skills to accomplish whatever they dream about. I want my music lessons to be more than boring old piano lessons!

"I want to change my students at their very core. I want my piano lessons to be a metaphor for life. I want my students to actually *care* about their success and, when appropriate, motivated by their lack of it. I want them to be excited and engaged. I want to inspire them. I want them to become self-directed, self-motivated beings of creation, able to create whatever they want!"

Silence. Ray just looked at me with raised eyebrows, "Is that all?" I might have imagined it, but I believe I saw a slight smile on the edges of his lips.

"Yes, I think …." I paused.

"Are you finished?"

"I think so."

But to me, it didn't feel like an ending, it felt more like a beginning, not the final wall of the house, but instead the first brick in the foundation. I felt so unstable with this outburst. But heck, he asked for it, hadn't he?

He looked at me more compassionately. "Knowing what you want is ninety percent of the battle to actually getting it. The first stage of creating any change is to create awareness, awareness of what you want. It's also an easy way to avoid what will not help you get what you want. Most people just complain about not having what they want, but never take the step of actually asking themselves what they want. Knowing what you *don't* want is fine but, ultimately, you need to refocus on what you *do* want."

Now it seemed like he was speaking in circles. He reminded me of the Zen masters who posed Zen koans to their students, unanswerable questions or stories that were simply told to get their students to think, like "What is the sound of one hand clapping?"

"Can you repeat that?" I asked.

"Knowing what you want also means that you know what you *don't* want. They are similar pieces to the same puzzle. I knew a professor who would give her students a perfect one hundred if they could answer every question on her fifty question multiple choice test with the wrong answer. They were not allowed to leave a question blank and if they could get *every* answer wrong, she would give them a perfect one hundred. If they got just one right, they got a two."

"Well, that sounds dumb," I replied.

"Really? Think about it. What do you have to know in order to get *every* single question wrong?"

"How to guess?" I responded, still confused.

"No, not at all," Ray replied. "As a matter of fact, there is a very high probability that if you guess you will get some answers correct and even if you got *one* correct answer on her test, you would not get a 98, you would get a 2! In order to get all of the answers wrong, the student had to *know how to avoid all the right answers*. The student had to know just as much to get a zero as he did to get a hundred!"

I changed my tune. "Wow, that takes a lot of guts. Did anyone ever do it?" I asked.

NICK AMBROSINO

"Only one student in that teacher's thirty-one-year career," Ray replied.

"Knowing what you *don't* want is as important as knowing what you *do* want. Knowing what you don't want, when you understand how to use that information, should create an immediate response for you to ask yourself, 'What DO I want?'" Ray repeated.

While I was considering what Ray had said, I looked past him into the next room and noticed an upright piano against the back wall. "Wow, what kind of piano is that?"

"I'm not exactly sure. I inherited it from a great aunt. Would you like to play it?" Ray replied.

"Sure, I'll take a look."

"It hasn't been tuned in quite some time, but I think it will be okay. It is, at least for me," Ray responded.

"I thought you said you didn't play?" I asked, as I walked over to the instrument.

"No, what I said was that I had never taken lessons."

"Hmm, a Chickering. Not a bad instrument. So, you do play?" I asked.

"A bit. I enjoy it. It's sort of like paint for my ears. When I was a young kid, I liked to draw with crayons. You know, just take out a color and make a circle or a line, just to see what the color looked

NOTES:

like. The sounds on the piano are like 'adult crayons' for my ears. I think of it as drawing with sound."

"That's a really cool, and un-teacher way of looking at the piano. I like it. Would you play something?" I asked.

"Actually, if it's okay with you, I'd rather have a professional like yourself play. The piano gets to respond to my amateur fingers all too often. I'm sure it would appreciate the finer touch of a trained musician."

I pulled out the bench and adjusted it to fit my five-foot-ten-inch frame. I played a simple scale to just feel the keys, and then I asked Ray if he had a favorite song.

"I've always loved anything by Chopin. I really like his nocturnes and sometimes use them to fall asleep," Ray responded.

"Well, you're in luck. I happen to be teaching a student the Chopin Nocturne in E Flat and I actually remember some of it," I replied.

I played the first two pages and when I had completed the second embellishment of the main theme, I looked at Ray and noticed that he had drifted off to another place while listening to the music.

"That is a beautiful piece, and I really enjoyed the way you played it," Ray said, as he mentally returned to the room.

NICK AMBROSINO

"Do you like classical music?" Ray asked.

"Yes, I enjoy all styles of music, but my favorite to play is jazz. I like the controlled freedom that is required when I improvise around the theme, sort of how Chopin adds more and more complex embellishments as he restates his original motif. It's almost like a jazz improvisation."

"Would you play a jazz piece?" Ray asked.

"Sure, how about, Gershwin's 'Someone to Watch Over Me'?"

"It's one of my Gershwin favorites," Ray replied.

I played through an entire arrangement of the piece, as Ray took a seat in the chair next to the piano. When I was done, the room remained silent, one of my signs that I had played well.

"You're quite an accomplished musician, Matt. You play with a lot of emotion," Ray said, after the energy in the room had returned.

"Thank you. I do enjoy playing."

"Did you know that your emotions are your GPS?" Ray asked.

"I'm not sure I'm following you," I said, confused.

"You play with a lot of emotion, but I wonder if you allow that emotion to guide you?" Ray asked.

"Of course, that's how I play with emotion. The emotion and the music are in a dance. Sometimes

NOTES:

the emotion creates the music and other times the music creates the emotion," I replied.

"That's interesting, but I wasn't referring to your music," Ray said, as he took out his iPad and jotted something down.

"Based upon your statement yesterday, about getting to my home, it appears you like to use your GPS," he continued.

"Yes, I do; it's usually pretty accurate," I replied.

"Well, do you realize that you already have a built-in GPS that's not 'usually pretty accurate' but always one hundred percent on the money, and that it will continuously and accurately point you in the direction of what you want?" he asked.

"What do you mean?" I asked, confused.

"Your body came with a built in, no subscription needed, GPS. It's been with you from the moment you were born and will continue to guide you until the moment you die. You know it by another name, 'gut feeling.' Haven't you ever had the experience where you know something is wrong but you don't know why? It just doesn't *feel* right?"

"Yes, but I usually ignore the feeling unless I can support it with proof," I replied.

"Most people do. Humans are trained to trust their logic and brains over their hearts. What they don't understand is that it's called your 'gut' feeling because it is Guidance U Trust or G.U.T. It's your internal GPS. The fact is, children and animals know how to trust their G.U.T. We're actually taught to pay less attention to that internal compass as we age. We're taught to think things through. We're mis-educated to believe our brain has all the answers. Young children and animals follow their instincts, their G.U.T. That's how I knew you had a good heart."

"What do you mean?" I asked, confused again.

"When you came into my home, Elvis immediately took to you. He didn't have to think about it or learn about your credentials. He knew on a G.U.T. level that you were okay. If you're good enough for Elvis, you're good enough for me. Congratulations, you passed the Elvis test," he said with a chuckle.

I wasn't sure if I totally bought into what Ray was claiming, but I could see his point. My initial visit to Jo's was because I didn't *feel* like sitting in my cold car. Without following that feeling, I never would've met Ray.

My next feeling was to return there after I didn't like the feeling of the seminar I was attending. I guess I returned to Jo's because first, I was nearby and second, I was comfortable there. It's funny though; *both* my internal GPS (my G.U.T.) and the actual GPS (in my phone) had pointed me towards Jo's.

"Feelings are your guide, your internal compass," Ray said, interrupting my thoughts. "For instance, let's say one of your students didn't practice. What do you usually do?"

COFFEE WITH RAY

"Well, I ask them why they didn't practice."

"And what does the student usually reply?"

"I was busy. I didn't have the time. I forgot."

"And do you believe them?"

"Usually not."

"Why not?"

"Because I once got so sick and tired of my students telling me this, that I did what any anal retentive, obsessive-compulsive, crazy music teacher would do ... I created a spreadsheet that accounted for every possible activity a child could have—eating, sleeping, school, sports, religious studies, other musical instruments, and even bathroom time!"

"You actually counted bathroom time?" he responded.

"YES! And time for goofing off, time for computer play, time for talking on the phone, time for ...."

"Okay, I get it. What did you come up with?"

"According to my calculations, everyone gets 1,440 minutes in a day or 10,080 minutes in a week. After subtracting all the time for the stuff I just listed plus *more*, I discovered a student *still* had 570 minutes a week for practicing! That's almost 10 hours!!! If they just practiced for 30 minutes a day or 210 minutes per week, they *still* had 360 minutes or 6 hours left to do anything else they chose! So you can't convince me that they don't have time to practice."

"I'm not trying to do that," he defended.

"I know, but I'm just saying."

"Well, be careful what you say. Your words are the windows to how you think."

The reprimand stung a bit, but I decided to accept his response so that I could move on with how to motivate my students to practice.

"So what happened? Did your student practice?"

"Yes … for one week. Then she 'forgot.' I started to feel like the old plate-spinning clown at the circus. I start on one end of the circus with one plate spinning then work my way to the other end to get all fifteen plates spinning only to have to run back to the beginning to provide some more plate-spinning energy to the first plate. I want my plates to spin on their own once I get them going."

Ray took out his iPad and again wrote something in it. "Log that as another thing you want. Good job, now you're getting the idea."

"Getting what idea? I was just venting," I exclaimed.

"I know that, but did you notice that once you stated what you *didn't* want, you immediately said what you *did* want? That is the secret to getting what you want."

NOTES:

COFFEE WITH RAY

Speaking to him can become dizzying at times! But he did sort of make sense.

"So, how do I get my students to 'spin their own plates'?"

"First, you learn what motivates them."

"You mean give them candy or stickers? I hate giving out stickers! And, once I do that, they'll have a way to *not* do something if I don't reward them. They'll have leverage on me. In addition, it also costs me money."

"And why is that not okay with you?"

"Because they shouldn't be trying to punish me by not practicing just because they didn't get a physical reward. They should be looking at themselves!"

"Perfect."

"Perfect? But how do I get them to practice?"

"Aren't you listening?" Ray said. "Feelings, you motivate through feelings. We all know that fear is a great motivator. History has proven this time and time again. If you can be the mean, stern teacher who gets angry when a student doesn't practice, you could motivate them that way."

"I don't like who I am when I do that."

"You mean you've tried it and didn't like the way it *felt?*" he asked with a raised eyebrow.

"Yes, at the beginning of my career. It only worked until the child was old enough to convince, annoy, or pester his parents to let him quit the lessons."

"Okay, so then the only way left to motivate them is through pleasure," he stated in summary.

"Pleasure? Are we back to the stickers and candy again?" I asked, wondering if *he* was listening to *my* original statement.

"No, you clearly stated that you didn't want to do that," he recanted.

"Oh good. I was just testing to see if *you* were listening," I joked. "So, how do I motivate them through pleasure?"

"Matt, people are either motivated to avoid pain or seek pleasure *or* when pleasure isn't a choice, to avoid the greater of two pains. These are ultimately the only two feelings. Some call them *fear* and *love*. Sure there are different intensities of these feelings, but when you boil all of your feelings down, they're either pleasurable or not. You've already decided that you don't want to motivate through the avoidance of pain, so that leaves you with only one option, to motivate by creating good feelings, pleasurable feelings. People are either motivated to avoid pain or move towards pleasure. You chose to be a *towards* motivator, not an *avoidance* motivator."

"That sounds a bit weird. Is that good or bad?" I asked.

COFFEE WITH RAY

"It's not a matter of good or bad. It's a choice, one that each person gets to make and one that each person can always change. Let me ask you a question," he continued. "How does it feel when you accomplish something you had to work at?"

"It feels good, really good. It's a great reward to me."

"Exactly! Accomplishment is its own reward. Or more accurately, the feelings you get from accomplishment are a wonderful reward. These feelings of accomplishment can become addictive because they're endorphin producing.

"Think for a moment about a time or event in your life when you felt proud, something you would share as an accomplishment. What was it?"

I immediately recalled riding my first century on a bike. A century is one hundred miles. A century to a cyclist is like a marathon to a runner.

"Do you have an event?"

"Yes, when I pedaled my first century on my bike."

"What was that like once you completed it?"

"Well, I felt I could do anything! I was flying high for days afterwards!"

"Okay, think of another event that created similar feelings for you."

"When I performed my senior recital in college."

"What did that feel like?"

NICK AMBROSINO

"When I completed it, the initial feeling was one of relief. But I also remember reflecting back on how insurmountable it looked at the beginning of my senior year. It was very difficult literature, and it all had to be memorized. I just never thought I could do it!"

"And therein lies the key!" Ray exclaimed.

"What key?" I was confused.

"The two events you just described, would you say they contributed to your self-esteem?"

"Absolutely! They helped me believe that I could accomplish anything I put my mind and effort to."

"Is it fair to say that both of them shared the feelings of fear and nervousness when you first started training for them?"

"Hmm, come to think of it, yes. I never really considered that."

"Yet, upon completion, they also both shared the feelings of pride and accomplishment?"

"Yes."

"That's the addictive feeling I was talking about. That's the feeling of growth, the feeling of expanding your comfort zone."

He lifted my coffee cup off the napkin on which it had been resting, removed the napkin from the saucer, and labeled the rings that had formed from the overflow.

NOTES:

COFFEE WITH RAY

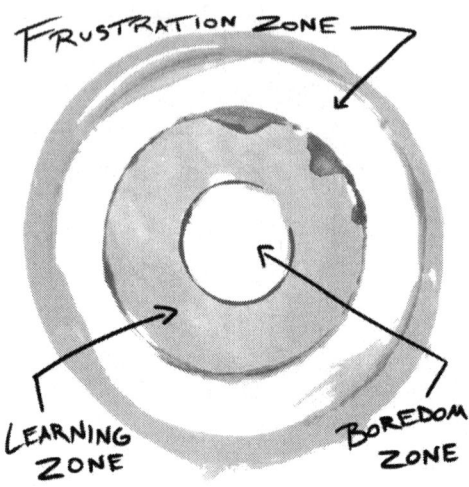

"The Boredom Zone represents all the things you can do. They really offer no reward except for that of comfort and safety.

"The Frustration Zone also offers no reward. It actually offers a penalty, the penalty of the feeling of frustration, which no one likes, but which we will talk about at a later time."

I wanted to hear more about the Frustration Zone now, because many of my students and I appeared to live in it, but I was beginning to accept that he would share information with me when he felt I was ready.

"The Learning Zone is where all the magic happens. This is the zone that offers you a bit of a challenge, but also offers a reward. A little bit of pain, but not so much to shut you down, and a good dose of reward to continue to motivate you.

Challenges in the Learning Zone are inviting without being too intimidating. Sort of like Goldilocks and the Three Bears."

"Goldilocks and the Three Bears?" I asked.

He just looked at me, pursed his lips into a small smile, and tilted his head. I knew that meant we would get to it at another time.

"So what you're saying is that a student should always be working in his Learning Zone? That seems pretty obvious."

"Sure, it's obvious, but how often do you see your students get frustrated?"

"Often," I sheepishly replied.

"Do you teach them how to deal with that frustration?"

"I don't know how to do that myself! How could I teach someone else?"

"Frustration is like coffee that is brewed too hot. If you permit me the analogy, it makes the learning 'bitter.' Once a person has reached that boiling point, his pot 'spills over' and nothing can be learned. The thermostat has to be reset or cooled off before you can proceed.

"The only thing you can learn when you're frustrated is how to deal with frustration. You certainly can't learn whatever it is that you were working on before you felt frustrated. The key to being in a successful learning process is to

COFFEE WITH RAY

constantly monitor your frustration, just like you would watch a thermostat on a coffee machine. You want to catch your frustration *before it hits the boiling point.*

"You can also see frustration like water in a bucket. It doesn't overflow and mess up the floor until the bucket is completely full. But, once it does, you need to clean up the mess on the floor before proceeding. Monitor the mental bucket before it runs over the top, and you'll always be ready to learn."

Wow, analogy after analogy, Ray was good, but he had more.

"Just as muscle fatigue is your body's way of telling you that the muscles are reaching their limit, so is frustration to your mind. Let's say you're exercising and your muscles start to send a pain signal to your brain. You can choose to ignore the pain signal. If you choose to ignore it, and continue working out, your body will increase the level of the pain. If you still continue to ignore it, it will eventually shut down that muscle.

"The same goes for frustration. Frustration is your mind's experience of pain. As you are working on a challenge, you may begin to experience a level of frustration, which is uncomfortable. Let's say a three or four on the pain scale. At that point, you might not choose to stop. You may choose to continue working on the challenge. If you don't successfully complete the challenge, your mind will increase the level of frustration thus increasing the level of pain.

"Let's say the level now reaches a six or seven and you *still* continue to ignore the messages your mind is sending, eventually your mind will continue to send increasingly higher levels of pain until the pain threshold peeks and you exclaim 'I can't do this!' You might even go so far as throwing your book and screaming, all because you didn't heed the warning that your mind was sending you, the warning that your brain was going on overload."

"So, what you're saying is that most people experience frustration as a stop sign, instead of heeding the yield sign that it actually is," I responded.

"Exactly. That's an excellent analogy. Maybe I'll use it someday!" he said as he reached into his back pocket, took out his iPad, and jotted down a note.

"You see, a person's feelings are always his compass, his map as to how to proceed. When you feel good, it's your mind or body's way of telling you to continue. When you consistently feel bad, in this context, the feeling of frustration is the "bad" feeling, it's your mind or body's way of telling you that you're not on the path of getting what you want."

"We're back to 'What do you want' again?" I asked.

"It all comes back to that! What you focus on continues to expand. If you continuously focus on

COFFEE WITH RAY

what you want, you will eventually achieve it. Think about it. Have you ever had a day that started out bad? You know, you stub your toe, your shoelace breaks, then you spill your coffee and you haven't even left the house? Did you notice that the more frustrated you got, the worse things continued to get?"

"As a matter of fact, I was having one of those days last Friday when I showed up at Jo's," I replied.

"The more you focused on what you *didn't* want the more you got it. Right?"

"Yes, I can see that."

"That's why you always need to be aware of how you're feeling. When a student feels bored, unless he *wants* to feel bored, he needs to increase the difficulty of the challenge. When he feels frustrated, unless he *wants* to feel frustrated, he needs to decrease the difficulty of the challenge. If, as his teacher, or more accurately his *facilitator,* you guide him to consistently adjust the steepness of his learning curve so that he's on a consistent path of success, you will eventually teach him how to 'spin his own plate.' This ultimately benefits both of you, as neither of you will feel frustrated and unrewarded."

"What do you mean by 'facilitator'?" I asked.

"Teachers tend to think about teaching a subject. When you redefine yourself as a facilitator, you become responsible for facilitating your student through the learning of how to teach himself," Ray replied.

I thought for a moment about all he had said. There was a lot to digest.

"So, in a way, frustration isn't really a "bad" feeling in that it lets you know that you're headed in the wrong direction. It lets you know what you don't want," I replied.

"Yes. A more accurate word, in place of 'bad,' would be 'uncomfortable' or 'undesirable,'" Ray clarified.

The thought of facilitating a student to become internally motivated was appealing, but it certainly didn't sound easy.

"That sounds like a tall order," I replied.

"It is, but is it what you want?"

"Yes," I replied with a bit of caution, reminded of a saying I once heard: be careful what you wish for because you just might get it.

"Would you like to get together again?" Ray asked.

"Sure. Are you available tomorrow?" I replied.

"No, I won't be around again until Saturday. Can you meet me at 10:30 AM?"

"Sure," I replied. "Here?"

"No." Ray said as we walked to the door. "Let's meet at Baseball Heaven in Harborville, just off

COFFEE WITH RAY

Route 25A. I'm helping out a friend of mine who coaches a local baseball team and Saturday is his first in-door practice. I don't believe I need to give you directions, as I'm sure your GPS will tell you where to go," Ray said with a touch of sarcasm.

Elvis had followed us, tail wagging. Ray turned to him and said, "We'll go out for a walk in a bit Elvis." Elvis' ears perked up and his eyes widened. He clearly knew what that meant.

I reached down and scratched his head. "Goodbye, Elvis. Thank you, Ray. See you Saturday."

"You're welcome, Matt. Enjoy your week."

Chapter 6

The rest of the week, I was distracted. I was looking forward to meeting Ray on Saturday, and I kept reflecting on the abundance of information he had shared with me on Wednesday.

I thought about feeling like the statue but remembered I had the freedom to move, and let my G.U.T. lead me by simply asking myself what I wanted.

As I went through my lessons with my students, I started to see them in a different light.

Many of them got frustrated at the drop of a coin and had absolutely no strategies or skills for handling that feeling. Interestingly, I felt a bit frustrated about their feeling frustrated.

First, I had assigned them a challenge that I thought was appropriate. Yet, based upon their feelings, specifically the feeling of frustration, many of the assignments appeared to be too ambitious. I started breaking the challenges down a bit more so that my students weren't in the Frustration Zone but, instead, were in the Learning Zone.

NOTES:

COFFEE WITH RAY

In one lesson, I broke the challenge down too much and could see the look of boredom on the young student's face. I decided to ask the student if he felt the challenge was too boring or too frustrating. When he responded "Too boring," I asked how we could make it less boring. Amazingly, he came up with his own challenge that he felt was appropriate. He then went on to accomplish it, and he looked proud.

When I left that lesson I didn't feel like a piano teacher, I felt like a facilitator.

Second, I realized that I didn't know how to teach my students the tools or strategies to handle the frustration they felt. For most of the week, I just told them to stop doing whatever was frustrating them. For many of my students, this meant completely changing my assignments for them. I felt like I was in unchartered territories without a map or GPS and couldn't wait to speak with Ray on Saturday.

Saturday came all too slowly. In anticipation, I didn't sleep well on Friday night. I felt like a kid on Christmas Eve. On Saturday, I got up early, had my cappuccino, rode the stationary bike, and showered. I hopped into my car and typed "Baseball Heaven, Harborville" into my GPS. The address came up as 110 Diamond Drive. Cool name for a baseball place. I hit the button that plotted the course and started on my way.

When I arrived, the place was much larger than I had expected. The parking lot was full and children of all ages were leaving and entering the facility. I entered the waiting area where I saw Ray talking with some younger baseball players.

"You made great contact when you kept your shoulder up during set up, Kyle. I'm excited about how well you hit when you did this," he said to one player.

"Thanks, Coach!" young Kyle replied.

"I like the way you were keeping your eye on the ball as it hit the bat, Connor," Ray said to another.

"Thanks, Coach!" Connor exclaimed as he ran to his father.

As his son ran to him, the father smiled, waved to Ray, and with a tone of respect said, "Thanks, Coach Ray ... for everything."

"You're pretty popular around here," I said as Ray and I made eye contact.

"They are the future of this world. My generation has done the best it could. Yours will too. Then after that, it will be up to these kids to create a better world."

"I'm not so sure my generation has made or is making the best decisions," I said defensively.

"Given the information they have, everyone always makes the best decision for themselves at the time they're making that decision. A moment later, with new information, they may be able to make a better decision but, at the moment they made the initial

NOTES:

COFFEE WITH RAY

decision, it will always be, *at that moment*, the best decision."

"Do you really think that's true?" I questioned.

"I never say something that I don't believe is true, so yes I do believe it's true."

We walked through the waiting room and into the facility which was a miniature baseball diamond surrounded by batting cages. There were batting coaches in the cages working with kids of all ages, five-year-olds up to high school students. In the baseball diamond, there was a coach working a double play drill with some students who looked to be about eleven years old.

"I like the way you kept your mitt on the ground so the ball didn't go under it," the young coach said to one of the players.

Ray caught the coach's eye and smiled.

As we passed a batting cage, I heard a coach ask a student, "What do you think happened on that swing?"

The student replied, "I wasn't balanced."

"Excellent! I like the way you're paying attention to your balance and position. Nice job!" replied the coach.

"This is a really positive way of teaching baseball," I said to Ray.

"If you're going to teach, why would you do it any other way?" he replied.

"Well sometimes you get frustrated teaching," I said.

"Who gets frustrated?" Ray asked.

"Well, I do."

"And whose problem is that, yours or your student's?"

"Hmm, I never thought of it that way. Mine, I guess."

"That's exactly right, Matt. The problem is yours, for whatever reason, probably because you don't know what else to do to reach the student," Ray said.

"Actually, that's pretty accurate," I replied.

"Many teachers, because they don't understand 'problem ownership' take their own frustration out on their students," Ray answered.

"I've been coaching baseball for a long time. I played through college and got drafted by the San Francisco Giants in 1963. I ended my career three years later when I met my wife. I didn't like how much the travel kept me away from her. I'm glad I did because we were only together for twenty-nine years before she passed away.

"I'm sorry to hear that," I replied.

"Thank you. She was an absolutely incredible woman and there isn't a day that goes by that I don't miss her," he said, fingering the ring around his left pinkie. The pain in his voice was evident, as was his adoration and love for her.

"When I was a ball player, the one thing I always noticed was that the most effective coaches weren't the ones who belittled their players in the attempt to make them become better. That's counterproductive. How can you belittle someone in order to build them up? Everyone likes a compliment or, even more specifically, a validation. People grow best in an environment that is supportive to their growth. Once the weeds enter the garden, they take over and eventually choke out the flowers."

"What do you mean by validation?" I asked.

"A compliment can be blown off by the person receiving it. For instance, if you tell someone who doesn't believe in himself, 'That's a nice shirt,' he will tell you, 'Oh this, my mom got it for me,' or 'Oh, it was on sale.' Almost as if he doesn't have the ability to pick out a nice shirt for himself.

"Validations stick more to the person, even if the person's self-esteem isn't one hundred percent."

"What do you mean?" I asked.

"What you're actually asking me to explain is what I have found and continue to look for in my life. I call them Diamond Distinctions."

"Is that why we're meeting at a baseball diamond today?" I asked, a bit sarcastically.

"Yes! You noticed that! I'm getting more impressed by your powers of observation," Ray said.

"Thanks."

"That was a validation. I told you how I felt about something you did. I validated your actions or results. How did you feel when you heard my validation?"

"Actually, I felt proud because *you* liked the way I noticed the baseball diamond symbolism."

"Remember that feeling. Validations tell how I feel about what you did. They are better than compliments which can be empty statements like 'That was good' or 'Good job,' which don't have anywhere near the impact.

"All the young coaches at this facility are trained to use validating feedback to bring out the fullest potential in their players. Validation is one of the primary distinctions my staff uses."

"What do you mean 'my staff'? Do you own this place?" I asked.

"Yes. My friend and I are partners. We opened it because we were tired of hard-nosed coaches taking their own frustrations out on their players. The coaches here have been chosen and trained because they're committed to an environment that brings out the best in everyone, in both themselves and the young players. They share both passion for the sport and compassion for the player."

COFFEE WITH RAY

"Wow, I never would've thought that such ideas would come out of baseball coaching," I replied, astounded.

"We're not just baseball coaches, Matt, just like you're not just a piano teacher. Being a baseball coach or a piano teacher insinuates that baseballs and pianos need to be taught. We are coaches who facilitate people on how to play baseball. Just as you coach, or facilitate, people on how to play the piano. It's the person who is important, not the activity. And there, is another Diamond Distinction.

"Diamond Distinctions are things that appear to make a small difference, but in actuality they create a major difference in effectiveness. As you start to pay attention and become more present in your teaching and your life, you will start to notice more and more of them. You will start to create them on your own.

"Remember Wednesday when we were speaking about frustration not being a *bad* feeling but instead an *uncomfortable* or *undesirable* one?" he asked.

"Yes," I responded.

"Well, that was another Diamond Distinction. Diamond Distinctions create a greater accuracy in communication and understanding. They also mentally re-label the feeling into one that is more easily dealt with. Many people see these Diamond Distinctions as just semantics, but I disagree.

"When you reset the paradigm of a word, you reset how the mind and body react to it. On Wednesday,

NICK AMBROSINO

you used the analogy of a yield sign versus a stop sign. That's exactly correct. You could also see them as red lights versus yellow or green lights.

"Think about the word *bad*. It has so much judgment and resistance attached to it. Yet the word *uncomfortable* or *undesirable* is more easily manageable. There is less internal emotional resistance, so it's a better choice."

As we continued our walk around the batting cages, we stopped in front of one coach who was working with a teenaged player.

"I like the way you made contact with that pitch, Mike, and now you're ready to turn your back foot." The student smiled and nodded. The coach threw another pitch and the student made solid contact. He looked back at his foot, saw his heel off the ground, his weight properly balanced and smiled with accomplishment. The coach caught Ray's eye. Ray nodded knowingly.

"What was that exchange about?" I asked Ray.

"That coach is one of the trainers for our other coaches. His name is Dominic. That student had been working with another coach outside of Baseball Heaven without much success. The coach's concepts and diagnoses were accurate but, and that's an important word here, his presentation of what Mike had to fix was not presented in a way that encouraged Mike to change.

"We assigned Mike to Dominic because I knew I needed to get this student on a quick path to

NOTES:

success before he quit. Dominic is a master of positive communication, and he just demonstrated an important Diamond Distinction."

"I must have missed it," I replied.

"The distinction was between the word 'and' and the word 'but.' Did you notice that Dominic said to Mike 'AND now you're ready to turn your back foot'?" Ray asked.

"Yes, it sounded a little odd."

"Odd or new, Matt?" Ray challenged.

Not willing to give up my point, I responded, "Odd because it was new."

"Okay. We'll get back to *that* distinction later. The point is that if you validate someone's performance, as Dominic did, and then you use the word 'but' to create a change in the performance, the student never remembers what came before the 'but.'

"If, however, you use the word 'and' as the invitation for change after the validation, the student feels he has earned the right to go onto the next part of his training and he will both remember the validation AND create the change."

"Wow, that sounds powerful! I've never even considered it. Come to think of it, I remember teachers telling me things like, 'Matt, you played it well, BUT you missed the G in the third measure and had a bad fingering on the second page.'"

"And how did you feel?" Ray asked with raised eyebrows.

"Crappy! It was like no matter how much I practiced, I was never good enough. There was always something to fix," I reflected.

"Exactly! You *feel* as though there is always something to fix. While that may be true, the word 'but' creates a feeling of 'less than.' It creates a closed condition for learning as well as an 'undesirable' feeling. The word 'and,' however, creates a feeling of greatness, of progress. It creates an opening for learning and that is a much more desirable feeling," Ray clarified.

As we continued our discussion about Diamond Distinctions, Ray and I stopped at the refreshment stand. I said to him, "This is a lot of stuff to think about. It's going to be hard to get this into my teaching."

"Now that's an interesting distinction, Matt," Ray said.

"I don't believe I made one," I replied.

"No, not yet. You just stated the first half."

"Are you going to clue me in or do you want me to guess?" I responded.

"You said that this was going to be *hard*."

"Yeah, it will. It's a lot of information."

NOTES:

COFFEE WITH RAY

"Hard is a *stop* word, not a *yield* word. Think of how the word *hard* feels to you inside. How does it feel to your G.U.T.? Do you feel like you're motivated to take on the challenge or do you feel resistance?"

"Well, when you put it that way, I'd have to say resistance," I replied as I said the word to myself.

"That's correct. *Hard* is a red-light word," Ray said.

"Well, what's a better word?" I asked.

"You see, Matt, the word *hard* isn't really accurate. It's just a knee-jerk reaction that most of us have when we start something *new* or *unfamiliar*."

"Hmm, *new*, *unfamiliar*. Yes, that's more accurate," I said, again repeating these new distinctions in my head.

"What if you simply said that the information was new and would simply take you time to assimilate or learn? How does that feel?" Ray asked.

"Well, it feels gentler. It doesn't have the pressure of the word *hard*. It's more ... inviting," I replied.

"Exactly! *New* is a yellow- or green-light word. That's the purpose of Diamond Distinctions, they make the learning more inviting," Ray said, smiling.

"You see *everything* you have ever learned was once *new* to you. Everything you have ever learned was once *unfamiliar* to you. Walking, brushing your teeth, tying your shoes, multiplication tables, playing the piano, hitting a baseball, the list goes on! Everything you have ever accomplished was at one time outside of your comfort zone. Yet, by labeling it as *hard* you put a question mark on your ability to learn or accomplish it. By labeling it as *new* you never question your ability but, instead, actually acknowledge that you are capable."

"Wow, that's huge! I hear students say that all of the time. I can see how, for my students, changing that one word will completely change how they see each new skill they learn!" I replied, excited by this distinction.

Ray just nodded and smiled.

An hour and a half had flown by, and I felt I had learned more in that time than in an entire semester of my college education classes. As we left Baseball Heaven, we stopped at the exit. Snow had started to fall.

"If you'd like to get together again, I won't be around this week, but I'll be at Jo's a week from Monday," Ray said.

I checked my calendar on my smart phone. "I think that will work. So, Monday the 3rd. Would 10:30 work?"

"Perfect. See you then. Enjoy your week," Ray said.

I walked across the parking lot to my car and Ray pulled out of his parking spot. As he did so, I

NOTES:

COFFEE WITH RAY

noticed the license plate on his blue Jeep Wrangler … it said, "Coach."

Chapter 7

To make sure I got "my" seat, I arrived at Jo's early. I was also excited to share with Ray all that had happened. The drive over was actually enjoyable, as the sun was shining and the temperature was a crisp forty-three degrees. The air smelled fresh with a hint of spring.

The place was empty except for three workers cleaning up the coffee machines behind the counter. One of the workers appeared to be senior to the other two, both in terms of her status at the café and her age.

When I walked up to the counter, she greeted me with a welcoming smile, "Good morning, Matt. Espresso or coffee this morning?"

I didn't recall ever being introduced to her. I noticed her nametag. It said *Camille*. I immediately checked my shirt for a nametag, none. "Excuse me, how do you know my name and coffee preferences?" I asked.

"Oh, I noticed you talking to Ray the past few times you were here. It's also part of my job to

NOTES:

COFFEE WITH RAY

make customers feel welcome. That's why I remembered what you ordered when you were here last."

"You know Ray?" I questioned.

"Of course. Ray is our boss, but he doesn't really like it when we refer to him as our boss. He feels that we all work together to create a common goal—a comfortable place for people to enjoy a good, albeit too hot, cup of coffee. Ray creates a very supportive environment for all of us to work and grow," Camille responded.

"Oh, he told you that the espresso was too hot for me?" I said, embarrassed.

"Yes. And he shares your sentiment. Ray spent a lot of time traveling and tasting coffee throughout the world. His favorite espresso is in a little café in Verona, Italy. He also loves Turkish coffee."

"You said Ray is your boss. Does he own Jo's?" I asked.

"Yes, he does."

Ray owns Jo's. Wow! First Baseball Heaven, now Jo's. What other businesses did Ray have his hands in?

"Then who is Jo?" I asked.

"Jo's Café was named after Ray's late wife, Josephine," Camille replied.

I wanted to know more, but felt uncomfortable asking Camille for Ray's personal information. I figured that if Ray wanted to share that with me, he would do so. But, before I realized it, the words had left my mouth.

"You said late wife. What happened to her?"

"Josephine passed away from breast cancer almost twenty years ago on May 2nd. Sometimes you'll see Ray wearing a pink ribbon in remembrance. Josephine was also my best friend. Ray always runs in the Breast Cancer Fundraiser Runs and donates ten percent of all the profits from Jo's to the Breast Cancer Foundation. If you look at the life preserver above, you'll notice a pink ribbon at the top."

I suddenly felt an uncomfortable and sad feeling in my stomach because of the loss of Ray's wife and Camille's friend, and because I had criticized both the price and temperature of the coffee in front of the owner. As I was lost in thought about my comments, the door to Jo's opened and Ray entered.

"Good morning, Matt! Hello Camille! I see the two of you have met," Ray said, jubilantly.

"Good morning, Ray. You're in a good mood. Did you go for a run this morning?"

"Absolutely! I would never miss a run on a crisp February day. It was invigorating," Ray exclaimed.

What are you in the mood for today?" Camille said with a smile.

COFFEE WITH RAY

"If it's okay with Matt, how about a French press of the Costa Rican Tarruza we just got in on Friday?" Ray asked.

"That's fine, whatever Costa Rican Tarruza is," I replied.

Ray extended his hand to our table. "Would you like the seat against the wall?" Ray asked.

"Thank you," I replied with a knowing smile.

"So, how was your week, Matt?"

"Fantastic, confusing, frustrating, and exciting!" I replied.

"Wow, that's a lot of stuff. Want to share what happened?"

Just before I was about to start, Camille brought over the French press, cups, and creamer.

"Thank you, Camille," Ray said.

"You're welcome," she said as she went back behind the counter.

"Camille has been here since we opened," Ray said, matter-of-factly.

"She said you own the place," I replied.

"Yes, I do. I built it after my wife passed away. We loved our coffee. We did a lot of traveling and couldn't wait to get to a new city or country and try out the coffee. No two cups were the same. Coffees are like snowflakes or people.

NICK AMBROSINO

"When my wife died, my life went dark. I withdrew from everything. It lasted for many years. She truly was a light for me. Building Jo's was both a therapy for me to move on as well as a way for me to keep her alive in the spirit of the community in which she taught. It's been a lifesaver for me. That's why there is one above the counter."

"Your wife was a teacher?" I asked.

"Yes. She taught sociology and psychology at the local high school and community college. She was adored by her students. I always said that she had the patience of a saint. She used to reply that she didn't have patience at all. What she had was *understanding* and, when you have understanding, you don't need patience. I guess that's another Diamond Distinction. Many of the books on the wall were from her library," Ray stated. He plunged the French press down and poured the coffee into our cups.

"Do a lot of your philosophies come from your wife?" I asked with caution.

"Yes. But the greatest gifts she provided to me, besides her love, were those of awareness and intuition, which I labeled Guidance U Trust ... G.U.T.

"Women feel things in ways men are not so sensitive to. You've heard the term woman's intuition?" Ray asked.

"Yes," I replied.

COFFEE WITH RAY

"Well, it's true. A woman tends to trust what *feels* right to her and men tend to want to have a good logical reason for trusting that feeling. She taught me to just trust. In so many ways, that one concept has opened my life. Trust in the good in people, trust in the good in myself, and trust that it will all work out. You are just responsible for the continued effort. The gentle power of trust can be more effective than muscle.

"You see, Matt, before I met Josephine, I was one of those coaches who belittled my players. Like you, I didn't like who I was when I was that aggressive angry person. Sure, I got results, but the results were based upon fear, not enjoyment."

"I understand what you mean," I replied.

"So, do you want to share more about your fantastic, confusing, frustrating, and exciting week?" Ray asked as he poured a drop of cream in his coffee.

"Overall, I was excited to try out my newly found strategies with my students but found that my reaction time was slow," I said.

"What do you mean slow?" Ray asked.

"Well, I usually figured out what to say or do *after* I left the lesson. I would be in my car and then the right words would come, but obviously too late. All of this new information and insights are great, but I feel incredibly overwhelmed. I feel like the only thing I've gained so far is an awareness of everything I *don't* know," I said.

NICK AMBROSINO

"That's because, on the learning curve, you're now between consciously unskilled and consciously skilled," Ray replied.

"What do you mean?"

"There are four stages to learning. First is being unconsciously unskilled."

"You mean like *ignorance is bliss*?" I asked.

"Sure, I guess you can think of it that way. I don't know if I agree with the bliss part, but I can accept that interpretation of unconsciously unskilled. You simply do not know what you don't know.

"The second stage is being consciously unskilled. This is where you're aware of what you don't know, but do not yet have the strategies to become skilled or may not choose to become skilled in that particular area. For instance, I know I don't know how to do brain surgery, but I also choose not to learn that particular skill.

"The third stage is being consciously skilled. This is probably one of the most frustrating stages because this is where you're aware of your mistakes, but you need more time to execute the solution. In this stage, your greatest assets are patience and kindness ... to yourself. This is a stage of work."

"That's what I experienced this week. I was working with a student when a situation came up that I didn't quite know how to handle. I knew that what I was doing was not the best. It simply didn't

NOTES:

feel like the absolute best solution, but I'm sure it was the best solution *for me* at the time I was doing it," I said, laughing.

"Now you're catching on! You just described the experience of being in the consciously skilled stage. With attention and practice, you'll move into the final stage, which is one of mastery. It's called *unconsciously skilled*. This is where you don't even think about your response. Your accurate responses are simply executed without thought. This is the stage where things feel effortless."

"I can't wait to get to that. It sounds much easier than where I am right now."

"Yes, it is. But remember, be patient with yourself. Without a doubt, you will become unconsciously skilled as long as you continue to reflect and be aware of the results of your interactions. It's just like hitting a baseball. When you're first learning, you spend so much time thinking about the mechanics that you usually miss the ball. But once the mechanics are in place, there is no thought when you see a pitch coming at you. You simply see it and swing.

"Did you notice anything else that was noteworthy to you this week?" Ray asked.

"Sure, plenty of things! Like I said, I actually felt and continue to feel overwhelmed. Last Saturday, you mentioned something about a person's self-esteem. It made me think, what exactly is self-esteem?"

NICK AMBROSINO

"That's a great question. Back in the 70s, there was a huge self-esteem movement in education. Basically, it said that if you continued to tell children they were great and everything they did was great, they would turn out great. But that's not what actually happened.

"The problem is, very simply, that sometimes things we do are not always great! Sometimes we simply do it wrong; we make mistakes; we screw up. Instead of those students learning that, what they learned was that learning was about never messing up, and that was not reality."

I remember reading something about this recently on one of my late-night tangential searches on the Internet.

Ray continued, "Those students never learned that *true* learning means messing up and then working past those obstacles to ultimate success. It means working on something you could not initially do, something that looked bigger than you, and then mastering it. That's how a person gets self-esteem. If you are truly learning, you're in the Learning Zone, not the Boredom Zone, which ultimately means you're going to stumble and make mistakes."

"Oh, something that has always bothered me now makes sense," I shared.

"What's that?" Ray asked.

"Whenever I saw one of those signs outside a preschool or in an advertisement for a music school that read, 'We make learning fun!' it always annoyed me. I never felt that learning was fun because it meant that you had to mess up and then fix it, then mess up, and then fix it. The process of learning was actually stressful, not fun. It's mastering what you learn that actually feels good. The product of learning, which is mastery, is what feels good."

Ray reached into his pocket and jotted a note in his iPad. It was starting to feel like a reward to me. When I said something that appeared to be noteworthy to him, he jotted it down.

"Excellent point," Ray said.

He continued, "It's called self-esteem because no one can give it to you. You have to earn it yourself. And the only way to earn it is to work on something that at first seems bigger than you and then, ultimately, to accomplish it."

"So *that* was the feeling I felt when I did my senior recital or when I rode my first century?"

"Yes! It was the feeling of growth, of you creating self-esteem for *yourself*."

I suddenly had a flashback to a student I had worked with at the beginning of my career. "Now something else makes sense!" I exclaimed.

"What's that, Matt?" Ray asked.

"Back in the beginning of my career, I had this student who didn't believe she could accomplish the song I had put in front of her. I knew she could.

NICK AMBROSINO

"I decided to work her through the steps of accomplishing the piece. I encouraged, I motivated, I convinced, I played the role of cheerleader—'You can do it! Yes, you can! If you can't do it, no one can!'—I gave her suggestions and asked her carefully planned questions to lead her to success. 'What is the name of this note? Try it again and use your second finger on the G. Try it slower. Now do it with separate hands. Great, now try it with your hands together. Now let's add in the feeling and emotion.' By the end of the lesson, she played the piece! I was super proud!

"When I looked at her, however, she didn't seem proud. As a matter of fact, she appeared even more depressed. I asked her if she felt proud and she shook her head. I couldn't believe it! We had accomplished the unaccomplishable. Why wasn't she proud?

"Why aren't you proud, Gina?" I asked her.

"Because I didn't do it, you did it for me. See, I was right; I'm not good enough to figure it out and do it by myself," she replied.

"Talk about good intentions backfiring! I was literally blown away! I didn't know what to say. Now I understand. I actually *contributed* to her low self-esteem because I had inadvertently convinced her that she was *right* about not being good enough to do something herself. Instead of facilitating her through her fears, I muscled her through them ... with my muscle, not hers. She had not taken

NOTES:

ownership of the challenge. I had. It was my success as a teacher, not hers as a student."

"Great insight, Matt," Ray said. "Another distinction you can pull out of that interaction is that *you* cannot get a student to learn. You can only provide an optimal learning environment in which the student can either choose to learn or choose not to."

"Isn't teaching about getting people to learn things?" I replied.

"Sure, you can look at it that way, if you see yourself as a teacher. Or, you can recreate your mission and see yourself as a facilitator or educator of people. Did you know that the Latin root for the word *educate* is *educare,* which means *to bring up?*"

"I think I might have heard that in one of my college classes," I responded.

"Nowhere does it say 'to force up.' Just as you cannot 'force' a plant to grow, you also can't do that to a student. Well, actually, you can, as many teachers do, but it's really not in the best interest of the student. You can only provide the optimal environment in which your student can choose to learn and grow. The responsibility to learn is up to the student."

"Well, that's not what most of the parents of my students see. They hold *me* responsible for their child's success or failure at the piano," I defended.

"Well, you do harbor a part of that responsibility," Ray replied.

"Oh, I get it, one-third to the student, one-third to the parents, and one third to me?"

"Well, that's one way of looking at it, but not quite what I had in mind. Everyone is always one-hundred-percent responsible. Relationships are not fifty-fifty. If they are, they're destined for failure because each person in the relationship is only willing to go fifty percent. All successful relationships are successful because everyone involved assumes the position of one-hundred-percent responsibility. In the case of you and your students, there are Three Responsibilities. If you're one-hundred percent responsible, it's up to you to create an environment where the Three Responsibilities are clear," Ray continued.

"What do you mean by the Three Responsibilities?" I asked, confused.

"When a student doesn't accomplish a goal, it's because one of three things happened. The first could be that the student didn't put in the effort. If this is the case, the student is one-hundred-percent responsible for putting out the effort. The student may enlist the assistance of his parents to remind him or help him set up an effective time management schedule, but the responsibility for this effort is one hundred percent in the student's hands."

COFFEE WITH RAY

"Well, that's great to know! I can't wait to use that on my students!" I exclaimed.

"It bothers me that you use the words 'use that on my students,'" Ray replied.

"The ideas I share with you are not so you can manipulate your student to do what you want but, instead, to assist you in creating a path that is best for your student, not one that is best for you. If *your* ego is what you're interested in growing, then your focus is not on your student. A true facilitator takes pride in his student's accomplishments, not in his ability to get his student to accomplish. That's a really important Diamond Distinction."

His gentle criticism stung a bit, but I understood what he meant.

Humbled, I asked, "What is the second responsibility?"

Ray paused, looked at me, and then proceeded. "The second reason a student doesn't accomplish a goal is because he doesn't have all of the information to do so. If this is the case, the responsibility lies on the facilitator to provide all the necessary information for the student to create a feeling of success for himself. So, that would be *your* responsibility."

"That makes sense," I responded.

"The third reason a student doesn't achieve a goal is because the goal was too big or too much. In this case, the responsibility lies in the hands of the student-facilitator team to create a more appropriate challenge. This is where the Three Bears story comes into play."

"Great! I've been waiting to hear this since you mentioned it the other day," I replied.

Ray continued, "While you may be able to present the next steps in a student's education, the learner is ultimately the only one who knows if he's ready to take all, some, or none of those steps.

"When you've discovered that the responsibility lies in the hands of the student-facilitator team, it's up to you to present the challenge AND up to the student to decide if that challenge is, in the words of the fable, 'too hard, too soft, or just right.'

"Remember the comfort zone picture I drew for you the other day?" Ray asked.

"Yes, I do," I replied.

"A challenge that is too hard, in the eyes of the learner, will only yield the feeling of frustration. A challenge that is too soft, or too easy, will yield the feeling of comfort and eventually boredom. A challenge that is just right will be scary enough to entice and motivate, without being so scary as to intimidate. Ultimately, only the student knows what kind of challenge this is."

"Sure, that makes sense. But what about the student who takes advantage of this and continues to choose challenges that are always comfortable to him because they're the easy way out? How do I get that student to grow and learn?" I asked.

"You show them how to be directed by their feelings. Share with them that while taking a challenge outside of their comfort zone might feel a bit scary, once they accomplish it, they will feel proud. The 'scary' feeling is actually a great sign. It's the sign that increased self-esteem is on the way.

"It's not a simple process to show a student how to be internally directed and how to use their G.U.T. as their compass for success. Many students are taught that making a mistake means they're not smart enough, not good enough, blah, blah, blah. When, in fact, making mistakes simply means that you need to try again because you're *growing,* which means you're learning. While this reconditioning is not simple, it is of extreme importance if that student is going to learn to succeed.

"It's sort of like breaking in a new pair of shoes. They're uncomfortable and stiff at first, and then with each step they become more supple and comfortable."

I felt information overload again; my mind was numb.

"Is it too much for you?" Ray asked.

"No, I think any more and my brain might explode, but I think I can process this with some time," I replied.

Ray just smiled and said, "Then go to it ... Goldilocks!"

I laughed as I realized he had modeled the whole process he had just shared with me.

When I looked down at my smart phone, time had simply flown by. It was already 12:30, and I had to go home and get ready for my day of teaching.

NOTES:

Chapter 8

Throughout the next week, I worked with my students with a renewed sense of excitement. I explained to them that learning was tough, but that didn't mean they couldn't do it, it just meant it would take work—work from them, work from me, and work from us as a team. Many of them responded with a mixed sense of wonder, confusion, and relief. Apparently, no one had ever told them that before. Some just looked at me like I was from another planet!

I started to teach them strategies for dealing with frustration in a healthy way. I read somewhere that you teach what you need to learn. Boy was that ever true for me now.

I continued to be on the lookout for more Diamond Distinctions that cleared the resistance in my students' learning paths and, as I did, I started to discover that being more accurate in how I chose my words also helped me to be more effective.

Instead of telling my students what they should do, I offered suggestions and asked them to take

NOTES:

responsibility for choosing goals that felt best for them. Sometimes they chose very simple goals only to return the next week and say that the goals were boring and should have been bigger. Sometimes they chose goals that were too big and came to the next lesson recognizing that they felt frustrated and needed to make the goals more manageable and achievable. The key was that they were guided by their own internal GPS, their G.U.T., their feelings.

The greatest thing that happened over the next few weeks was that I felt less stressed out and frustrated and my students started taking responsibility for their own learning. They were actually beginning to spin their own plates!

One student in particular, Jessica, really seemed to get it. When I arrived at her lesson and I asked her what she had accomplished this week that she felt proud of (I found that to be a better and more effective way of starting the lesson than asking them if they had practiced.) She said, "Nothing."

"Nothing?" I repeated.

"No. I didn't make time to practice this week because I had too many tests and projects due in school."

Wow! What a key statement she had made. "I didn't *make* time to practice." Not "I didn't *have* time to practice." She was accepting complete responsibility for her actions and results. What more could I ask for?

NICK AMBROSINO

I complimented her on her choice of words. She smiled and asked, "This week, could we practice together in our lesson?"

"Absolutely," I replied.

I was extremely busy over the next month, as I started to write down some of the Diamond Distinctions that were really working as well as some of the ideas Ray had shared with me. I even came up with my own. Funny thing was, with as much as I love technology, I went out and bought a small "iPad" that I could keep in my back pocket to write down the ideas that came to me, just like Ray.

Strangely, I started getting more calls for lessons (ten in two weeks) and decided to find another teacher to work for me. The interview process was unfamiliar (I reminded myself it was not too hard!), and I plodded my way through it. I did find one young lady, Diane, who was willing to join me in my mission of changing the world one music student at time.

Several weeks, later, on a Monday toward the end of March, I returned to Jo's. Winter had clearly passed as the wild croci were starting to bloom.

As I drove to Jo's, I had to put on my sunglasses as rays of sunlight shone brightly through my car's windshield. I walked into Jo's fully expecting to see Ray sitting at our table waiting for me. But Jo's was empty, except for two workers behind the counter. I looked down at the time on my smartphone, 10:26; I was early.

NOTES:

COFFEE WITH RAY

I walked up to the counter, and I was greeted with a smile from Camille. "Hi, Matt. How are you today? Long time no see."

"Great, Camille! What time do you think Ray is coming in?" I asked.

"As a matter of fact, Matt, he's out of town. He won't be in today," Camille replied.

"Will he be in tomorrow?"

"I don't know."

"Do you know when he'll be back?" I asked.

"No, I'm sorry," Camille said.

"Can I get you a cup of coffee?" she asked.

A million questions were running through my head, but all I replied was, "Yeah, sure, double espresso please."

Camille pulled the espresso shot into a thick ceramic cup that was brown on the outside and white on the inside, placed it on a small saucer and pushed it across the counter to me. As I reached for it, she reached under the counter and pulled out a plain white, letter-sized envelope with my handwritten name on the front.

"Ray left this for you. He had wanted to mail it to you, but didn't have your address. He told me that the next time you came in to give it to you."

NICK AMBROSINO

I slowly reached across the counter and took the envelope. I grabbed the saucer below the coffee cup with my left hand and made my way to "our" table.

I sat down, back to the wall, able to see all angles of the café, fully expecting Ray to walk in. He didn't.

I took a sip of my espresso, opened the envelope, and pulled out the handwritten tri-folded letter. The letter was written on a piece of fine letterhead. The ink on the page was clearly put there with a fine-tipped fountain pen, the thick and thin strokes giving away their source.

My Dear Friend,

While you may see yourself as a teacher of the subject music, you are so much more! You are a teacher of people; that is your true specialization, not just the subject of music. Yes, when students come to you, they want to learn a special set of skills but, as an imperative compliment to that specific skill set, you teach them how to learn, how to grow. What an incredible gift that is!

NOTES:

COFFEE WITH RAY

Every profession has a set of tools that needs to be mastered in order to master the job of that profession. The job of a master teacher is to consistently create a learning environment in which your student can achieve his or her greatest potential, both as a learner of the subject and as a person.

What are the tools in your tool chest that help you do your job and accomplish your mission? What are the tools of a master teacher? Which tools do you use to create an environment in which your students can create their own successes?

As a teacher, you do not have to be compassionate, nice, firm, exciting, stern, humorous, energetic, quiet, serious, entertaining, inspiring, or funny. What you have to be is <u>effective</u>, which ultimately means you are all of the above! As an effective teacher, you are a chameleon. To be effective, you need to know what tool to use to get the job done.

A master teacher is a conglomerate of professions. You are a detective, a doctor, an architect, a psychologist, a coach, and a comic.

You are a detective because you have to find out what your student's learning challenges are.

You are a doctor because you need to diagnosis how to treat those challenges.

You are an architect because you need to design a blueprint for the success of your student.

COFFEE WITH RAY

You are a psychologist because you need to understand your student as a person.

You are a coach because all good coaches stay on the sidelines and "coach." They do not enter the game.

You are a comic because there will be times you will need to lighten the mood.

Many of your students will have the wrong idea about learning. They will have been told, by teachers and other authority figures who are well meaning but misled, that learning is supposed to be fun. This is simply not true.

Learning is work and, for the most part, work is not fun so, by proxy, learning is not necessarily fun. The feelings of accomplishment, success, and pride, however, are extremely powerful motivators. Showing a student how to create these for himself is a gift that will inevitably change that student's life forever. In the mastery of a task always lies the reward of pride, and pride is a much stronger motivator than fun. What an incredible gift to give them!

What is that gift, you may ask? It is the gift of growth, the expansion of their comfort zones. Once your students become addicted to that feeling, nothing will stop them from achieving their own personal greatness. It is in this greatness that not only the student grows but, on an even larger scale, the world grows as well. If each individual in the world is happy, the world will be happy.

What if your student holds the key to solving the world's hunger problem but does not believe or take pride in his own ability to learn? Do you think he will unwrap his gift and deliver it to the world? Of course not!

What if your student is a scientist-to-be who will eradicate the world of cancer, but he doesn't believe in himself? Do you think he will deliver his cure to the world? Absolutely not! He will continue to harbor it deep in the depths of his own self-doubt.

You are so much more than a subject teacher; you are an educator who shows people how to achieve their fullest potential. You are an educator who uses the learning of his subject as a metaphor for the learning of self and life.

A very important part of your job is ensuring that your students are not renting information from you but, instead, becoming "experience owners." The only way they can become owners is through work and effort. Do not rob them of this opportunity, for each time you do so you will also be robbing them of the chance to create self-esteem.

Someone cannot learn to ride a bike by renting the information about balance and forward momentum from you or a book. They must experience it for themselves! They must go ride a bike, inclusive of the falling and bruising that comes with the learning. Certainly, you can support them, but you cannot ride the bike for them. They must have the bike-riding experience for themselves. Similarly, they must have the experience of expanding their comfort zones for themselves, inclusive of the inevitable failures and bruising along the way. It is a mandatory part of learning.

NOTES:

COFFEE WITH RAY

Rest assured, on their path to success, they will stumble. This is when you need to reach into your toolbox and use the tool of compassion. To quote an overused but accurate adage, "People do not care how much you know until they know how much you care!"

Ultimately, this is what it is all about—to care enough about the success of those put in <u>your</u> care that you are willing to do whatever it takes to create an environment in which they can thrive. You don't just want them to grow; you want them to thrive! You want them to explode with the joy of knowing they can achieve anything they set their mind to!

Know this, if you are a good teacher, and it is clear that you are, few people will be as committed to your student's success as you. Sometimes this can feel frustrating and stressful. Do not resist the frustration for through your resistance you will only add fuel to its toxic fire. Acknowledge it as a sign of your commitment and desire for your student's success. Relax. Take a step back and choose a more appropriate gradient, a goal that is not too hard, not too easy, but one that is just right. Readjust your goal to one with which you can feel successful and which will create success for both you and your student. You both get to win!

We will meet again when the time is right for both of us. Thank you for the gift of your friendship. I am privileged to have had the opportunity to share ideas with someone so open-minded, as well as to have learned from you. You will thrive and, as a result, so will your students.

Yes, you taught me, too. No relationship is one-sided. People do not come into your life for you to either serve them or for them to serve you. Both parties are served by the relationship, both have gifts to unwrap and give through the relationship.

Until we meet again, look up; what do you see? How many times have you been to Jo's? Do you see the canoe hanging from the ceiling? It is now time to paddle it yourself.

Your friend,

Ray

I took a sip of my coffee; it was perfect.

The End

Made in the USA
Middletown, DE
26 February 2016